Traders panic in the New York Gold Room on Black Friday, September 24, 1869.

Cornerstones of Freedom

The Story of
THE NEW YORK STOCK EXCHANGE

By Zachary Kent

 CHILDRENS PRESS ®

CHICAGO

On October 24, 1929, crowds gathered on the steps of the Sub-Treasury Building across the street from the New York Stock Exchange when stockholders heard that the stock market had collapsed.

Library of Congress Cataloging-in-Publication Data

Kent, Zachary.

  The story of the New York Stock Exchange / by Zachary Kent.
    p.   cm. — (Cornerstones of freedom)
  Summary: Describes the origins, significant historical landmarks, and recent events of the New York Stock Exchange.
  ISBN 0-516-04748-5
  1. New York Stock Exchange—Juvenile literature.
[1. New York Stock Exchange.] I. Title. II. Series.
HG4572.K46 1990
332.64'273—dc20   89-25374
                                          CIP
                                          AC

PHOTO CREDITS

© Cameramann, Int.—2
Brown Bros.—22 (left)
Historical Pictures Service, Chicago—8 (left), 9, 12 (left), 13, 14 (left) 15, 17 (right), 23 (right), 25
Museum of the City of New York—11, 17 (left)
New York Historical Society—10
New York Stock Exchange—8 (left), 21 (right)
Northwind Picture Archives—1, 7 (2 photos), 12 (right), 14 (right), 19 (2 photos), 21 (left)
TSW-Click/Chicago © Jim Pickerell—32
Wide World Photos—cover, 4, 22 (right), 23 (left), 26, 29 (right), 30 (2 photos)

Total panic gripped the brokers on the floor of the New York Stock Exchange. For years these men had successfully traded shares of stock in American companies, driving up their values and making money for investors. Suddenly on October 29, 1929, however, the upward market wavered and stock values began to drop. As the word spread, investors nationwide hurriedly instructed their brokers to sell their stocks and save their profits.

"Sell at market! Sell at market!" shouted brokers at the trading posts on the Exchange floor. "They roared like a lot of lions and tigers," according to William Crawford, superintendent of the Exchange. "They hollered and screamed, they clawed at one another's collars. It was like a bunch of crazy men." Traders, clerks, and messengers crowded together waving slips of paper. At Post Number 12, where stock in the Radio Corporation of America (RCA) was traded, broker Ed Schnell said it seemed "the heavens had opened up. The stock was being pounded, down, down, right down . . . ."

Outside, crowds of people jammed into Wall Street anxiously awaiting news. By the time the market closed, the frenzied day had seen a record

16.4 million shares of stock change hands at a staggering loss of $10 billion in value. Thousands of investors had seen their savings wiped out in a single stroke. "WALL STREET LAYS AN EGG," blared the show-business newspaper *Variety* the next day. The Crash of '29 sent the national economy plummeting into the Great Depression—the darkest economic period in U.S. history. Many people blamed the reckless brokers who had gathered at Wall Street each day to speculate dangerously on stock prices. Others remembered, though, that the New York Stock Exchange also had provided Americans with many investment opportunities over the years.

The world's greatest financial district started as a small settlement in 1609, when Dutch traders landed at the southern tip of Manhattan Island. They named their settlement New Amsterdam. In 1653, Governor Peter Stuyvesant of New Amsterdam ordered a high protective wall built along an old fenced path at the outskirts of the thriving settlement. The British took over the community in 1664 and renamed the territory New York. In time, the road where the high wall stood became known as Wall Street.

Stretching from the East River's busy harbor to the Hudson River's docks, Wall Street was a natural

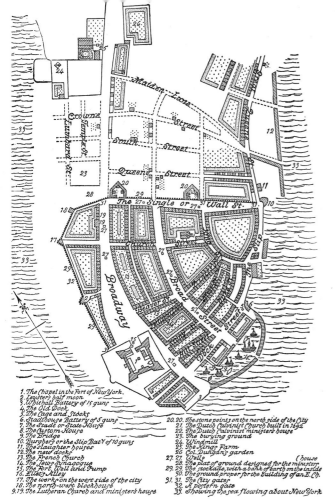

1. The Chapel in the Fort of New York
2. Leyster's half moon
3. Whitall Battery of 15 guns
4. The Old Dock
5. The Cage and Stocks
6. Stadthouse Battery of 5 guns
7. The Stadt or State House
8. The Custom House
9. The Bridge
10. Burghers or the Slip Bat.y of 10 guns
11. The slaughter houses
12. The new docks
13. The French Church
14. The Jews Synagogue
15. The Fort Wall and Pump
16. Ellet's Alley
17. The works on the west side of the city
18. The north-west blockhouse
9.19. The Lutheran Church and minister's house

20. 20. The stone points on the north side of the City
21. The Dutch Calvinist Church built in 1692
22. The Dutch Calvinist minister's house
23. The burying ground
24. Windmill
25. The Kings Farm
26. Col. Dungan's garden
27. 27. Wells
28. The plat of ground designed for the minister's house
29. The stockade, with a bank of earth on the inside
30. The ground proper for the building of an E. Ch.
31. 31. The City gates
32. A postern gate
33. Showing the sea flowing about New York

This map of the southern tip of Manhattan Island in 1695 shows the City of New York and Wall Street. The wall protecting the settlement was built of upright logs called palisades.

meeting place for merchants and traders. For a hundred years, businessmen gathered there to buy and sell cargoes of molasses, tobacco, and furs. Thousands of cheering Americans crowded into Wall Street and neighboring Broad Street on April 30, 1789, to witness General George Washington's inauguration as the first president of the United States. After fighting from 1775 to 1783, Americans had won their independence from Great Britain. As George Washington solemnly took the presidential oath on the balcony of Federal Hall on Wall Street,

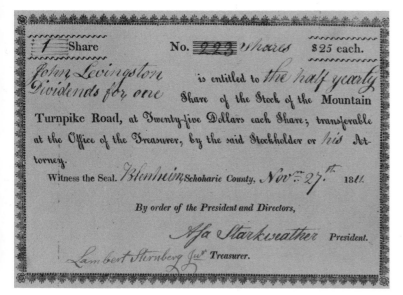

Left: A stock certificate issued in 1811 was used to help fund a road in upstate New York. Right: The Bank of the United States was founded in Philadelphia in 1795.

Americans prayed that their new nation would survive and prosper.

To pay Revolutionary War debts, the U.S. Congress soon voted to sell $80 million worth of bonds. Each bond certificate promised to pay a fixed sum at a future date. In addition, the bonds paid regular interest. The nation's first bank, the Bank of the United States, also wanted to raise money in order to expand its business. The bank's printing press soon produced stock certificates to sell. Each share of stock represented a small part-ownership in the bank. Other banks and insurance companies also decided to sell stock. These stocks and bonds came to be known as securities.

Wall Street was known as the center of fashion in 1789.

Throughout the Wall Street neighborhood, merchants, stockbrokers, and auctioneers gathered to trade securities. They conducted business at all times of the day wherever they happened to be—in their offices, in coffeehouses, and even on the street. As trading activity increased, New York's leading brokers recognized the need for an organized stock exchange. On May 17, 1792, twenty-four brokers assembled beneath an old buttonwood tree at 68 Wall Street and signed a document. "We, the subscribers, brokers for the purchase and sale of public stocks, do hereby solemnly promise and pledge ourselves to each other . . . ." The signers of this Buttonwood Agreement agreed to trade stocks

The Tontine Coffee House (building with flag) contained the stock exchange and insurance offices in the late 18th century.

only with one another and to take a commission, or small fee, from the individuals they represented.

In warm weather, the brokers usually conducted their auctions beneath the leafy buttonwood tree. On wintry days, the brokers often traded stocks in an upstairs office at the new Tontine Coffee House on Wall Street.

The Wall Street business district thrived during the next twenty years. As America's largest city and a center of commerce, New York seemed a perfect location for an active stock exchange. On March 8, 1817, exchange members adopted a formal constitution creating the New York Stock and Exchange Board. The constitution called for the

The Merchants Exchange building occupied an entire city block and cost over a million dollars to build.

election of a board president, regular meeting hours, and rules of conduct. In a private room at 40 Wall Street, the Exchange president called members to order every morning at 11:30. Stock in about thirty different companies was offered for sale at that time. One by one, the president called out the names of these companies. At each call, the brokers made bids to buy the stock or bargained to sell it. During the trading, each broker remained seated in his own chair. Ever since, the term "having a seat" has meant having a membership on a stock exchange.

Through the years, the Exchange moved several times to larger and more comfortable quarters. In 1827, the members began meeting at the Merchants

Stocks and bonds were used to fund booming transportation systems such as the Erie Canal, seen here at Lockport, New York, and the Mohawk and Hudson Railroad.

Exchange building. Sometimes trading was so slow that brokers fell asleep. On March 16, 1830, the quietest day in Exchange history, only 31 shares of stock changed hands. Increasingly, however, business boomed as the nation expanded. Companies planning to build new roads and bridges sold bonds to pay for the projects. Canal construction also excited many Americans. New York State, for example, sold $8 million worth of bonds to pay for the fabulous Erie Canal, which joined the Great Lakes with the Atlantic Ocean. The canal opened in October 1825. In August 1830, the Mohawk and Hudson Railroad became the first railroad stock listed at the Exchange. Other companies sold stock and used the money to lay rails across the country. Wall Street brokers smiled as trading grew to an average of 5,000 shares a day by 1834.

The great New York City fire of December 1835 destroyed the headquarters of the Stock Exchange.

Troubles plagued the stock market during the next few years, however. On December 17, 1835, great sheets of flame roared into the skies of lower Manhattan. The worst fire in the city's history destroyed hundreds of buildings—including the Merchants Exchange. In 1836, still housed in temporary quarters, the Exchange survived a disastrous panic. When the federal government closed the Second Bank of the United States, it sparked financial rumors and fears. Before the year was over, nearly 650 other banks had failed. New Yorker Philip Hone remarked, "The immense fortunes which we heard so much about in the days of speculation, have melted like the snows before an April sun."

Left: Samuel F. B. Morse, inventor of the telegraph. Right: Before 1872, stocks were auctioned individually at formal Stock Exchange meetings.

In time, the business community recovered from this depression. The clicking dots and dashes of Samuel F. B. Morse's new telegraph in 1832 allowed the Exchange to become a national securities market instead of just a local one. The smashing success of the United States in the Mexican War of 1846 to 1848 and the discovery of gold in California in 1849 filled American investors with renewed enthusiasm. Railroad stocks and bonds especially attracted buyers as the nation's rail system stretched toward newly settled lands. By 1857, trading volume on the Exchange reached as high as 71,000 shares a day.

Competing stock markets existed in New York throughout this period. Some merchants still traded stocks "over the counter" in their stores. Other New York brokers gathered in the streets of the financial district. Meeting at corners and beneath lampposts, their market came to be called the Curb Exchange. (After the Curb Exchange finally moved indoors in 1921, it was called the American Exchange.) The New York Stock and Exchange Board, however, remained the most powerful market and set the standard prices for securities. By raising initiation fees and limiting membership, the old established brokers ran the Exchange like a private club. Stockbroker Henry Clews recalled, "The old fellows were united together in a mutual admiration league, and fought . . . tooth and nail . . . when a young man

Brokers who were not members of the Stock Exchange did business on street corners in the "Curb Exchange."

sought entrance to their sacred circle."

The outbreak of the American Civil War in 1861 abruptly changed the style of the Exchange. President Abraham Lincoln solemnly vowed to keep eleven rebellious Southern states from leaving the Union. In the Northern states, factories and railroads quickly expanded to meet the U.S. government's crucial war needs. War fever triggered a great burst of trading on Wall Street. "The whole population of the North," remarked broker James Medbery, "gave itself up to a speculation frenzy. Brokers were overwhelmed with orders." Old Exchange members hired youthful clerks called "pad shovers" to help deal with increased business. Exchange membership also grew to meet demands.

Wall Street's brokers closely followed the progress of the war. Stock prices rose and fell with each victory and defeat on the battlefield. Giddy Exchange members burst out singing "John Brown's Body" when Union soldiers won a battle, or "Dixie" when Confederate troops scored a victory.

In 1863, the New York Stock and Exchange Board officially changed its name to the New York Stock Exchange (NYSE). The final Union victory in April 1865 brought relative calm to the reunited nation at last. However, continuing activity kept the Exchange busy.

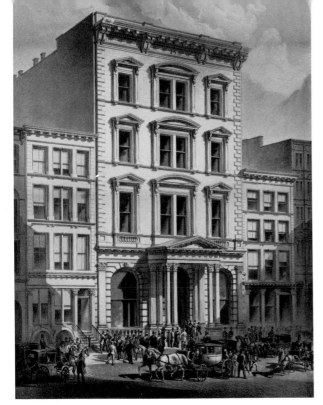

Left: The Stock Exchange building on Broad Street in 1865. Right: The stock ticker enabled traders to keep track of the latest stock prices.

In December 1865, it moved into its own new building at 10 and 12 Broad Street. Two years later, E. A. Calahan presented Wall Street with a new invention. His stock ticker spewed out paper tape reporting up-to-the-minute stock prices. In brokerage offices throughout the city, speculators eagerly gathered around stock tickers to get the latest information. On one occasion the ticker on the Gold Exchange broke down. Hurriedly, Exchange officials found a skillful twenty-two-year-old mechanic who made quick repairs. The young man, Thomas A. Edison, later proved himself a genius with such inventions as the phonograph and the incandescent light bulb.

The private club atmosphere of the NYSE began changing in October 1868, when it first allowed its brokers to sell their memberships. Seats sold during that year for an average of $7,500. In May 1869, the Exchange merged with two rival markets, the Open Board of Brokers and the Government Bond Department. This instantly ballooned Exchange membership to 1,060 brokers. The Exchange also adopted some new trading methods. By 1872, instead of holding the old-fashioned formal auctions, Exchange members preferred to gather in a large room and conduct continuous auctions among themselves. At different trading posts across the floor the brokers huddled to buy and sell shares of stock. One day, according to legend, a broker named Boyd arrived at the Exchange with a broken leg. Rather than hobble from place to place, Boyd chose to remain at one trading post and deal only the special stocks traded at that post. This trading method proved so successful that other brokers soon became "specialists" too.

As the United States prospered, so did the New York Stock Exchange. Telephones first rang at the Exchange in November 1878. Alexander Graham Bell's invention allowed brokers to call in their orders from their offices instead of sending clerks running through the streets to the Exchange. The

Far left: By 1881, brokers engaged in continuous trading on the floor. Left: Alexander Graham Bell uses his telephone.

market grew, and the Exchange reached its first one-million-share trading day in 1886.

In traditional Wall Street slang, brokers call a generally upward economy a "bull market." A generally downward economy is called a "bear market." The origins of these terms may come from the fact that bulls thrust upward with their horns while bears pull downward with their paws. Speculators often look for economic signals and trends to help them predict whether the stock market will be bullish or bearish. In 1889, broker

Charles Dow began publishing *The Wall Street Journal* to provide valuable financial news. Readers first studied his daily printed Dow-Jones average of industrial stocks in 1896 and thereafter used it to measure the health of the stock market. The huge successes of business leaders such as John D. Rockefeller of the Standard Oil Company and Andrew Carnegie of Carnegie Steel greatly bolstered the national economy during these years. Wall Street speculators made huge fortunes by trading stocks in the most popular companies.

Every investment remained a gamble, however. For example, in 1884 the collapse of the banking firm Grant & Ward ruined thousands of investors. Crooked broker Ferdinand Ward went to jail, while his cheated partner—the former U.S. President Ulysses S. Grant—declared bankruptcy. In 1893, suddenly collapsing stock prices sent the United States into its greatest financial panic yet. Millions of Americans lost money and jobs during the long depression that followed. In his 1894 book *The Tragedy of Pudd'nhead Wilson,* writer Mark Twain humorously warned: "October, this is one of the peculiarly dangerous months to speculate in stocks. The others are July, January, September, April, November, May, March, June, December, August, and February."

In the NYSE building at 18 Broad Street, brokers (right) used telephones
(booth at left) and stock tickers to keep up with the latest trading information.

On April 22, 1903, brokers loudly celebrated the
opening of a new NYSE building at 18 Broad Street
near Wall Street. Handsome carvings and six great
marble columns marked the front of the structure.
Inside, sixteen separate trading posts rose across
the great trading floor. Broker booths with
telephones lined the walls. High on two walls stood
electric boards on which the latest stock quotations
were constantly announced. These large boards may
have given the NYSE its nickname—the Big Board.

During the crisis of 1907, anxious investors crowded into Wall Street "as if to watch a fire." J. Pierpont Morgan's (right) decisive actions brought the panic to a halt.

In November 1907 one powerful Wall Street banker singlehandedly prevented a national financial panic. When selling by bearish brokers threatened to pull down the stock market, J. Pierpont Morgan quickly called a number of important bankers to his New York mansion. He insisted that together they must immediately pump $25 million into the stock market to keep prices stable. Through the night, Morgan refused to unlock his front door and let the bankers leave until everyone had agreed. Morgan's forceful behavior brought the panic to a halt.

The eruption of World War I in Europe in August 1914 created an international financial crisis. To prevent a stock-selling panic in the United States, the NYSE closed its doors for four months. In 1917, the United States entered the war. Soon, demands for ships, guns, and other war materials greatly expanded industrial production. Americans bought millions of U.S. Liberty Bonds to support the war effort. By war's end in 1918, the number of Americans who owned stocks and bonds had jumped from 200,000 to 20 million.

The United States emerged from World War I economically stronger than ever before and America

Vice President Thomas R. Marshall selling Liberty Bonds to a group of U.S. senators in Washington, D.C.

23

charged ahead into the Roaring Twenties. Booming sales in the automobile, radio, airplane, and motion-picture industries led the skyrocketing growth of the New York Stock Exchange in the 1920s. New stock issues rose from 1,822 in 1921 to 6,417 in 1929. Thrilled by the idea of making fast profits in this bull market, millions of Americans hurried to buy stock certificates. Broker Otto Kahn recalled, "the public . . . were determined that every piece of paper should be worth tomorrow twice what it was today." A popular business method used by investors was to buy their stocks "on margin." In this way, the investor paid only 10 per cent of the stock's price and the brokerage firm loaned the investor the other 90 per cent. Each day, the buying frenzy pushed stock prices to even higher levels.

By 1929, a few wise observers warned that prices had risen much too high. On October 29, the bubble finally burst. Stock prices started falling. On the Exchange floor, frantic brokers waved handfuls of sell orders in the faces of the specialists. Stock tickers could not keep up with the rapidly falling stock prices. Desperate brokers called investors demanding payment of margin loans to cover mounting debts. Investors sold stocks to raise money, pushing prices even lower. "Stock prices virtually collapsed yesterday," exclaimed *The New York*

Thousands of investors lost everything they owned in the stock market crash of October 29, 1929.

Times on October 30, 1929, "swept downward with gigantic losses in the most disastrous trading day in stock market history."

Millions of investors were ruined. Some committed suicide. As the crash continued, thousands of other investors wept as their savings disappeared. The value of stock in General Motors (GM), for example, fell from $92 to $7 per share by 1932. Hundreds of brokerage firms, banks, and businesses failed, as the nation faced the worst economic depression in its history.

Clerks in a busy stockbroker's office in the 1930s taking and giving orders. They used megaphones to make themselves heard above the noise.

Many Americans blamed margin trading and careless and unethical brokerage methods for the stock market crash. In 1934, the U.S. Congress created a new federal agency, the Securities and Exchange Commission (SEC), to watch over the stock market. To head the SEC, President Franklin Roosevelt named shrewd investor Joseph P. Kennedy. As first SEC chairman, Kennedy made sure that New York Stock Exchange trading rules were followed fairly and honestly.

On December 7, 1941, Japanese planes swooped down in a sneak attack on Pearl Harbor, Hawaii. America's entrance into World War II snapped the nation out of its long depression. While men entered the armed forces, women went to work at the NYSE for the first time as quotation clerks and messengers on the trading floor. By war's end in 1945, busy factories and bullish investors had started stock prices heading back in a very positive direction.

While Dwight D. Eisenhower served as U.S. president from 1953 to 1961, the stock market continued to rise. Bullish buying extended well into the 1960s and happy brokers called that period the Go Go Years. Of course, bad economic or national news sometimes sent the market plunging. For example, on November 22, 1963, the news that President John F. Kennedy had been assassinated caused panic selling. Stock values on the NYSE dropped $13 billion in less than an hour of trading.

Advanced electronics have helped the NYSE progress through the 1970s and 1980s. In 1976, the Exchange introduced a new superfast computer system. The Designated Order Turnaround System (DOT) sends orders from brokerage houses to the appropriate trading posts on the Exchange in seconds. The computerized StockWatch system also installed that year keeps track of every trade and checks for possible illegal activities. During 1980-1981, the NYSE greatly modernized its trading floor. Workmen installed seventeen new trading posts, each equipped to handle up to one hundred different stocks. Video monitors display up-to-the-minute trading information. Using these monitors, specialists, traders, and clerks can learn the latest stock prices at a glance.

Today, the New York Stock Exchange, the largest in the world, lists the stocks of about 2,250 companies. Even on slow days, over 100 million shares of stock change hands there. A seat on the Exchange sold for $550,000 in 1989 and 1,366 brokerage firms own memberships on the NYSE.

Other stock exchanges in the United States include the American, Boston, Cincinnati, Midwest, Pacific, and Philadelphia exchanges. Since 1978, a computer network called the Intermarket Trading System (ITS) has linked these exchanges to the NYSE, allowing traders to shop around for the best stock prices. American companies that are not listed on an exchange can sell stock in over-the-counter (OTC) trading through a computer system called NASDAQ. Worldwide, other large stock exchanges also operate in such cities as Tokyo and London.

Every day on the NYSE, the forces of supply and demand affect stock prices. Americans searching for stock investment opportunities carefully read the annual reports issued by companies. Business magazines and the financial pages of newspapers yield valuable economic information, too. Often the advice of stockbrokers also influences an investor's buying or selling decisions.

Anxious traders watched stock prices fall on the video monitors during the hectic activity of October 19, 1987.

Few people, however, predicted the great stock market crash of 1987. On the crowded floor of the NYSE on Monday, October 19, 1987, a downward slide in trading suddenly turned into an avalanche. "By 11:00 we knew we were going to have a new

During the October 1987 crisis, traders rushed to keep up with the wildly fluctuating market. By October 20, a newspaper was calling the stock market plunge a bloodbath.

volume record," said NYSE Chairman John Phelan, Jr. "There were orders from all over the country, and they were predominantly sell orders." Nervous brokers hurried from post to post clutching sell orders. So much stock changed hands that the over-burdened DOT system shut down four times, adding to the panic. At last the NYSE closing bell rang at 4:00 P.M. Stunned brokers gazed at video monitors and saw that the Dow-Jones average had dropped a record 508 points. Brokers had traded an astounding 600 million shares of stock. An incredible $500 billion in stock values had vanished in that single day. Chairman Phelan gravely called the Crash of '87 "a financial meltdown."

Many experts blamed automatic computerized selling programs, designed by investment firms, for sparking the crash. Luckily, the strong national economy bolstered trading through the next few days. Americans sighed with relief as the country avoided the horrors of 1929 and another Great Depression.

"Could it happen again?" an anxious writer later asked Chairman Phelan. "Sure," he answered. "You'll always have declines in the market, and every once in a while, you'll have a crisis."

Since brokers first stood beneath the buttonwood tree, the ups and downs of the stock market have reflected the moods and progress of America. "There is no investment which does not involve some risk and is not something of a gamble," famous Wall Street financier Bernard Baruch once remarked. The nearly 50 million Americans who personally own shares of stock today seem willing to bet on the nation's future. They watch with interest as Wall Street's bulls and bears struggle to triumph at the New York Stock Exchange.

Across from the Stock Exchange, a statue of George Washington commemorates the site of his inauguration as the first president in 1789.

INDEX

About the Author

Zachary Kent grew up in Little Falls, New Jersey, and received an English degree from St. Lawrence University. Following college he worked at a New York City literary agency for two years and then launched his writing career. To support himself while writing, he has worked as a taxi driver, a shipping clerk, and a house painter. Mr. Kent has had a lifelong interest in American history. Studying the U.S. presidents was his childhood hobby. His collection of presidential items includes books, pictures, and games, as well as several autographed letters.